CASTING A F

by

David Pattison

Typeset and published by
The National Poetry Foundation
27 Mill Road
Fareham
Hants PO16 0TH
Tel: 0329 822218

(Reg Charity No 283032)

Printed by
Meon Valley Printers
Tel: 0489 895460

© David Pattison 1991

Sponsored by Rosemary Arthur

Cover Photograph by Celia Rambaut

To Pauline

All rights reserved. No part of this publication may be reproduced, stored on a retrieval system, or transmitted, in any form or by any means, without prior permission of the publishers.

ISBN 1 870556 11 9

£4.00

CONTENTS

Casting A Faint Shadow	1
Wish You Were Here	2
We'll Take Good Care Of You	3
Viable Targets	4
Old Lady's Song	5
A Lady And Her Lover	6
The Free Spirit	8
My Eyes Play Tricks On Me	9
Mr Wonderful	10
Discovery	11
The Caretaker	12
Dance Class For The Over 60's	13
Birth Of A City Boy	14
At Cober Hill	16
The Woman In The Attic	17
Having A Few Words	18
Strictly For The Birds	19
At The Supermarket	20
Heard On The London Train 27-04-89	21
Four-Fold Death	22
The View From Fifty	23
The People Are Fine	24
Dreams Made Of Tar	26
At The Booksellers Fair	27
Mad Mickey	28
This Is The Estate	30
Just A Matter Of Time	32
Flight From The Gosforth Park Hotel	33
You're Looking Well	34
Mass Hysteria	35
Just Names On A List	36
A Soldier's Death	38
It Used To Go Like That	39
Now You Can Do All Of Those Things	40
In My Red Poppied Blue Mac	41
The Certificate	42

CASTING A FAINT SHADOW

They arrive unannounced
Those links with the forgotten past,
A sudden scent on the wind,
A touch, a sound, a taste,
Bringing memories of long ago.

Casting a faint shadow
That fades before it is known,
Leaving only the traces
Of unanswered questions.

WISH YOU WERE HERE

Through the porthole drawn on the steamy window
he watched the cloud shadows slide off the sea
to switchback swiftly up the uneven beach. Across
the promenade a stiff wind whisked cold salty air
against upturned collars as fine sand spiralled,
dancing over the sandalled feet of day trippers.

Blue hands clamped cardboard hats hard to deny
the greedy wind, underchin elastic needing extra
help. The door to the cafe opened allowing plastic
macs to scrape and rustle their way to shiny topped
tables where condiments trapped cards offering
fish, chips, tea, bread and butter for £1.50.

Grains stuck to the grease on his fingers as he
poked patterns of circles in the damp sand. Sitting
back on his heels he looked across at the cafe, above
it their holiday flat. He could see his mother
at the window. His father was at his elbow scraping
a channel in the sand. Smiling he watched as grey sea
water frothed messily over the dam before vanishing,
draining away to leave white edged traces of a thin
meandering trail of slowly bursting bubbles.

WE'LL TAKE GOOD CARE OF YOU

They say I am a baby
When I dribble down my chin.
They laugh at my damp trousers
When I can't keep water in

And when my head lolls backwards
As they drop me in a chair
They assume a sort of blankness
From my pale and moist-eyed stare.

To them I'm just an object,
A cripple they call Pop,
As they sluice me in the bathroom,
Wash my body with a mop.

How I long to tell them,
If I could make it clear
It's my body they are using,
I'm trying to live in here!

Although no words are spoken
The light still gleams inside
My spirit isn't broken
I'm still desperately alive.

Now I have no time left,
There is no one to blame.
The last words spoken of me,
"He's dead then, what's 'is name?"

VIABLE TARGETS

Dear Santa, thank you for your letter.
Why did you write to me again to send
A Pension Plan? I'm six years old.
Another man, one of your friends I think

Sent me a picture of blue sky and a house
With words and numbers I didn't understand.
You didn't send me the horse or the boat
But I did get a shiny book from someone

Daddy called Booper who will give me
Money when I'm ill. I don't like being ill.
Not even for money. I get lots of letters
From your friends. I don't like them much.

Daddy laughed and said I'm not a boy
I'm a consumer. I don't like that either.
This is my last letter, I'm nearly seven
Now, and too old to believe in you anymore.

(A recent news item revealed that children who had written to Santa Claus at his Greenland workshop received not only a letter from Santa Claus but, subsequently, unsolicited mail as they had been identified as 'viable targets' suitable for selling–by–post techniques)

OLD LADY'S SONG

It never used to be like this
Life was perfect, life was bliss
But things are very different
Nowadays.

The streets are full of Rastas
With their noisy ghetto blasters
And the shops are run by Pakis
Nowadays.

It's too dangerous after dark
Only rapists play in the park
And the police just sit in cars
Nowadays.

The family have all gone
Sometimes they telephone
But we're left living all alone
Nowadays.

Chains and bolts on every door
Put there to make us feel secure
But there's nothing left to live for
Nowadays.

Watch the telly, read 'The Sun'
Count the bruises every one
We're just so much copy
Nowadays.

A LADY AND HER LOVER

Around the hall excitement
As the band began to play
The dancers hesitating
For two to lead the way.

The caller's voice went soaring
Good humour filled the air
The caller now imploring
Four couples to a square

Gipsy boy chase gipsy girl
By the fiddler's frantic beat
You've caught her boy!
Give her a whirl!
The floor shook beneath their feet.

Creaking bones were lightened
As the evening wore on
Then old muscles slowly tightened
While the music tore along.

Two didn't miss a single dance
Although both past middle years
They stepped and crossed,
Went promenade
and laughed themselves to tears.

Alone, among the others,
They danced with everyone there
But they never left each other
This unique and fortunate pair.

And when the dance was over
They walked home, hand in hand
A lady and her lover,
And the music of the band.

THE FREE SPIRIT

I'm a free spirit, he said
as the alarm clock insisted
he get out of bed,
to stand in line
for the six thirty nine.

I'm a free spirit, he said
as the siren sent him out
then called him back
without using his name.

I'm a free spirit, he said
paying his dues to sick club,
health club, union and queues
of government departments
claiming rights on his life.

I'm a free spirit, he said
as the landlord cried, Time,
and he hurried home
to reset his alarm clock.

MY EYES PLAY TRICKS ON ME

I need two pairs of glasses now,
one to read with, the other to help
me pose as I gaze unseeing
into the middle distance; as poets do.

That line or half moon on bi-focals
is not for me, it makes things jump
when you move your head, the way trick
photographs have pretty girls wink
as you move the card from side to side.

Contact lens never did suit, a cricketer
of my acquaintance lost one on the field,
we watched him search for it,
on his knees, in the rain.

I'll stick with two pairs of glasses.
When I wear the wrong pair and stare
people will think me intense and poetic,
but I will be just trying to see
what I know is already there.

MR WONDERFUL

People admire the things I do
– I'm sick of it. *You're
writing poetry? At your age?
How marvellous!* they coo
before returning to security
to tut and shake their heads
and think that I am mad.
*How sad – he's doing an
'O' level now,* they whisper,
Maths – whatever next?
With unmalicious mirth they rush
to watch my antics professing
admiration but seeking
ammunition to confirm that
I am mad and they are sane
to carry on with the day by day
turmoil of travelling from here
to there to earn the price
of the fare. I don't care
for their admiration or
the look in their eye
that gives a lie to the words
that are spoken. I don't care
for their supposed support that
merely undermines and smiles
at the forecast of collapse. I do
what I do, that's enough.

DISCOVERY

The evening had a chill about it
that made a jacket welcome after
a warm, shirt sleeved day. The Tynemouth beach
was shadowed flat as the sun sank
into the North Sea. Its final rays
streaking gold across the high blown clouds,

splashing pink on the wings of the gulls.
Small dark waves boiled white in mock anger
at my feet before sucking swiftly
through the pebbles to safety. My parents
were sitting side by side on
the promenade wall as I walked alone
at the sea's edge. It was August,
1953, I was twelve years old.
There was a song in my head.

THE CARETAKER

Why are you so cold, old woman?
On a warm summer night, fastened
Into your wheelchair with a brown
And yellow blanket. Your sensible
Grey coat fastened by other hands
Which tucked your hands away and
Pulled the hood up over your head.
You could be dead in there. Who is
That pushing your chair? His mind
Is in another place from yours.
I see you trundling by my window
Two lone shells on a distant shore.

DANCE CLASS FOR THE OVER 60'S

"Forward, side, together and..."
Sweating couples strain and pull
Each other against the rhythm
Of the dance.

"Smile, you're here to enjoy..."
Bald heads gleam with tension
As glasses glint reproach
At each false step.

"You won't learn sitting..."
Hopes boosted as a couple
Sit down in mute anger
At an uncloseable gap between

Brain and feet.
White knuckled fingers
Clutch and tear at shoulders
And backs as the music beats

Over the heads of the dancers.
"Interval please..."
Tension free tongues meet
"Yes that's a lovely dance –

I'll have a gin, small one –
No, I've never sat down – it
Might be my favourite. We'll
Really get it next time."

During the interval music
Plays, but no one dances.

BIRTH OF A CITY BOY

I've always been a City boy at heart.
The country is fine but it is difficult
To be solitary with no one around
To protect yourself from. I remember

The reversed time on the face of the
Coloured Guinness clock in Paragon Square
Shining up at me from black wet streets —
Automatically my shoulders hunch, my hands

Go deep in my pockets as I remember the lone
Walks through the winter of the deserted town
— The emptiness suiting my mood. Most of all
I remember being aged about five years old,

Watching the snow slanting past the street
Light at Bate's Terrace end. The silence
Was complete and all was black and white
Except for the suggestions of colour from

Fletchers shop and the circle of light
Thrown by the lamp. The snowflakes drifted
Through the circle and then settled on the street.
Cars were a rare sight then and I watched

The dark streets speckle with white
Then thicken undisturbed. Odd patches clung
To the houses turning them into pebbled
Cottages. Here and there I caught sight

Of a slice of light escaping through
Black-out curtains to tint the snow briefly
With yellow. Above my head the still warm roofs
And chimneys partly resisted the advance

As the fall drifted down onto the most
Perfect silence I had ever known.
I've been a City boy ever since.

AT COBER HILL

The soft sprung turf supports my head
As I look up through the circle
Of trees. The clear evening sky
Pale and darkening to the east.

Behind me a male voice droning
Heaney. Larkin gets a female
Voice to give him a fighting chance
With his sky-high airborne rivals.

This is almost perfect. There are
Some almost friends sharing the
Moment: knowing only who I am,
Not caring who I was. By turning

And squinting I see 1850,
Carved in stone above a door.
How very sure of permanence.
The brick is honey coloured, worn,

Touch warm. By standing I can see
Down the lane to the sea and catch
Sight of the slice of brilliant
Yellow on the cliff top. The lane

Bumps halfway down over a one
Time railway, now a dark, secret
Path, tree cowled, mysterious.
There is a single magpie.

I hold my breath until I see
Another. A robin lands near
My feet, so sure and unafraid.
This is almost perfect.

THE WOMAN IN THE ATTIC

A late Victorian pile of stones
That was once a merchant's home,
And is now a dozen separate slices
Of life sharing a communal hall.
I am to see the woman in the attic.

She never pays but I need the cross
In my book to prove that I called.
The passage light is on a time delay,
I flick and run. At the second landing
I lose to the night and stumble, now
Guided by the voice of her crying child.

There is no other sound; no sight at all.
But there is the smell. The smell
Of nappies, dogs and cabbage –
Always cabbage. The baby cry wraps
Me in its reeds and tries to drag
Me down. The thin note doesn't change

As the attic door opens, revealing
The smooth face of the mother, "Shut up,"
She coos to her child, "For fucks sake,
Shut up." Turning to me she murmurs,
"Fuck off," and quietly closes
The door, leaving me in darkness.

HAVING A FEW WORDS

From a distance they could be taken
For the lovers that they used to be.
They are standing close together. She is
Leaning forward, animated. He is quiet,

Head bowed and attentive as her fingers
Puncture the world around him
With sharp jabs of accusation.
He is trying to keep intact under

The corrosive attacks. Her spittle
Acid tongue splashes the gap between
Them with words that melt flesh. Valium
Used to comfort but now only contrasts

The voided with the vicious. Her lips
To his ear, soft hair brushing his cheek
In what was once a lovers gesture,
She threatens to die.

She is always threatening to die. One day
The ritual promise will become sacred
Rite and she will be gone; leaving
Him alone with his whisky and his women.

STRICTLY FOR THE BIRDS

At the age of seventeen,
Convinced I had a way with words,
I decided to write a novel, called
'Strictly for the Birds'.

It was going to be about Life,
Leavened with the heady despair
Of youth and the secrets we had found
In our desperate search for Truth.

I never wrote more than the title
Before I went down a different road,
To become unique with all the others,
Watching the years unfold.

I wonder if I should write it now,
Add all the things I've seen?
But as experience stacks up behind me
The less it all seems to mean.

AT THE SUPERMARKET

At the supermarket, although cautious,
And after several practice runs, I always
Pick the trolley with the wobbly wheel.
Or perhaps it picks me. I am deceived

At first as it rolls arrow straight.
Then, when it is fully laden, it crashes
Into shelves, children and old ladies
With tartan shopping bags on rubber wheels.

My arms ache with the strain of battle
As the beast lurches, desperate to answer
The destructive siren call of towers
Of high stacked tins of baked beans and

Marrow fat peas. Forcing it down narrow
Gangways raises my blood pressure,
And the pencilled eyebrows of the flat
Faced cashier, who takes my money

And gives me to freedom. The trolley,
Empty now, is taken from me by a blank
Eyed youth who rolls it with one hand,
Arrow straight, to the trolley park.

HEARD ON THE LONDON TRAIN 27-04-89

A capricious child at three is a delight,
But at twelve it's a bore and by fifteen
A nightmare. She has her freedom,
If she doesn't like what we do
That's fine. I tell her, Lydia,
You needn't eat that food but there is no more
Until tomorrow. As for homework, I've told
All three, It's up to you, I will tell you
Only where to look, after that it is for
You and your conscience. It's your life.
All three have their freedom, I've seen
To that. They choose what to do, if it
Doesn't fit in then they can go somewhere
Else. I have my life to lead. They were
Such lovely children but they have grown up
Sullen and difficult. I can't understand
Why that should be, they have complete freedom
To do whatever they want to do.
As long as they clear it with me first
And it fits in with everybody else,
They can do what they like. They used to be
Such lovely children but it's different now.

FOUR-FOLD DEATH

I saw death four times last Thursday afternoon
On my two hour business trip around the town,
Four black caravans crawling their resolute way
To appointed meeting places, crossed my path.

Not that it upset me. Death always belongs
To someone else. I had glanced at my watch
To know when they would be tear gulping songs
As the boxes slid through the curtains.

Why four? It's been weeks since I saw any.
Perhaps the gravediggers or the stokers
Have been on strike and now the boxes are
Stacked and circling like tourists above Heathrow.

I don't know. But all day long a farmers song
On planting seeds in fours kept coming back,
First sung to me by Horace Shillittoe when
I was van boy to his driver many years ago.

"One for the rook and one for the crow
One to rot and one to grow." For all I know
Horace was one of the four. It would please
Him that I remember that silly little song.

THE VIEW FROM FIFTY

My years will number more than fifty
The year I clutch my degree and graduate
Towards a different life, but now I begin
To wonder, have I left it all too late?

But those who know, no more than four,
Will argue back at me that I had no choice
In the matter. I had to make the break
Or continue screaming with the silent voice

That would have led me into the darkness.
Remember those harsh, white bright glimpses
Into hell? Promising hope, peace and release,
Mistaking the call of death for Freedom's bell.

Those days are gone. Packed with the business
Suits in polythene bags and hung in the closet.
Only taken out every once in a while
To be examined with a half remembering smile.

No, the timing was just right. I had to become
What I was then so that I can be what I am now.
When my years number fifty my life will be three
Years old. A very experienced, very young man.

THE PEOPLE ARE FINE

Night after night the awful sight
Of shiny, shapeless, graceless death
Flickers into my life, as The News at Ten
Or the Nine O'Clock News, screen
Slickly packaged disturbing views
In two minute chunks. "Son of a bitch!"

The samaritan screamed as her beak torn
Finger bloodied the oily feathers.
The grave undertones of the voice-over
Whisked me to another theatre
Of some sort of war before my two minute
Interest waned. Of course Chernobyl upset me.

Lockerbie too, although that only killed
People who happened to be there
Or were just passing through.
Up in the Arctic, deep in the Exxon oil,
It's only animals, birds and fishes
Passing through, or just being there.

The images of the people are fine.
Oil black waves will last longer
Than the haunting memory of them.
Soon, when the world is dead
And we live protected lives in domed cities
We can watch the screens all the time.

Visions of forest and jungle, white sand,
Green grass and tall waving hedgerows,
Clean clear air alive with bird song.
We will smile and tell each other of the way
Life used to be. That will be so much easier
Than caring about how it is now.

DREAMS MADE OF TAR

Summers were much hotter then.
I remember when the tar
Bubbled in the streets.
Small domes wearing dusty grey caps.

Beneath the dull outer skin
The deepest, shiniest blackness.
We collected great gobs,
Sucking up the rich smell,

Rolling the tar into hand sized balls,
Throwing impossible catches
To each other with the smell
And feel of summer days.

Once I collected the roundest
Blackest sweetest smelling ball.
Dreaming to make a thousand marbles
I took it home.

Next morning the small globes
Shattered into tiny pieces,
Hard, sharp and separate,
Smelling of nothing at all.

AT THE BOOKSELLERS FAIR

First with heads upright
then on one side to read
those awkward titles written
down the spine, the bargain
hunters move crab like
along the rows of books.

Suddenly a hand darts out
quick as a lizards tongue;
a book is hauled in
to be stroked and fondled.
Pages persuaded open for
a penetrating mind.

Too often rejection follows,
the book slipped back
to await another. Meanwhile
the search continues.

When a match is made
the couple leave together
to conduct
a most private affair.

MAD MICKEY

Known as Mad Mickey he never spoke
to those who shouted out the name.
Always at the same place, every day,
on the way home, an out-patient now,

proud he'd found the secret
of control. Coat fastened tight
with two belts to hold the fright.
Everything about him taut as he fought

to stop his stride from becoming
a wild unstoppable charge.
Gloveless hands blue cold
with fingers stiffly straight

down the line of his arms
held angled from his sides. The rigid arms
balanced by his unmoving head;
a triangle to grip his body.

He knew that if arms or head moved
he would lose control and run
until he was exhausted and lost.
His hair was cut too short, unevenly spiky,

showing the muscular throbbing bulges
in the temple above his ears.
The too blue distant eyes
deep etched with pain and power

glowing with the battle for his mind.
Without warning a stone came with
the shouted name. Making him turn,
releasing his arms,

breaking the triangle. Years of
screams tore from his throat
as his angles lost their corners.
Then he began to run.

THIS IS THE ESTATE

Cut off from the town by the river and the fear
Of being different, the houses are built
Where children once took a penny bus ride
To breathe country air. This is the Estate.

Papers, polystyrene cartons and empty crisp packets
Gather in dusty hedge bottoms.
Every now and then the wind collects them
To throw each piece high in a frantic spiral.

The wide sweeping roads all meet at a Court
Or a Close, never a street; they vanished
With the slums and the memories and the shop
On the corner with its bell on the door.

Some gardens straggle a few flowers here and there
But most are bare, paper strewn and dog littered.
The houses show only faded faceless red brick.
There are no people to be seen.

There are people there, behind the curtains, the walls
And the Government statistics. But not to be seen.
This is the Estate. This is where people go to brain die.
Where the dogs are half mad and run in packs.

Where the schools are always half empty of children
And completely empty of hope. Where the shopping centre
Has barred windows and notices shouting 'No Credit'.
Where no credit has ever been due.

This is the place of old men and old women who remember
But forget what they remember, only that it was better then.
This is the place where the police patrol in pairs
And never get out of their cars.

This is the place where the buses don't run after dark.
A place of graffittied subways and unlit walkways,
Brightly lit doorways and double locked doors
On the houses that will never be homes.

This is the Estate. Once the way forward
To the city in the skies but now just
A reminder of political lies. Where a different sun
Shines with no warmth at all.

JUST A MATTER OF TIME

I had been waiting at the hospital
For several days and nights,
Unnoticed now by the nurses
As I stood by the bed
Near the window.

Behind me the slow pulse of breath
From the worn and weary body;
In front of me a well worn lawn
And some daffodils.

It seemed an age that the lifeless
Clock had ticked on. Not recording
The advance of time but rather
Its retreat.

The bright red and grey of a robin
Flashed as he landed on the window sill.
I saw his beak open but heard nothing
Through the glass.

He looked into the room,
One eye at a time,
Then flew away. Behind me
The clock had stopped.

FLIGHT FROM THE GOSFORTH PARK HOTEL

Replacing the telephone silence
Overwhelms me.
Down the corridor voices
Murmur and open doors
To each other. My room is silent.
My other voices far away.

I know that outside in the blackness
Release is waiting.
A cocoon of light that will hurtle
Through the night. Or I could stay here
And watch the dirty film
On Channel Eight.

Holding my small black case I watch
The red numbers flick floor by floor
Across the row.
The lift doors hiss open and fumbled
Gropings become giggles
At my presence.

I enter the bright white light
Of the foyer –
Soon welcomed into the safe
Sheltering blackness of the night.
I'm going home.

YOU'RE LOOKING WELL

The thin reedy baby cry
wavered and nagged constantly.
It had been a difficult birth
for such a poor little thing.

All pinched and puckered skin
with an old man's face
and an unsure grip on life
its crying ebbed and flowed
but never stopped.

The mother had wanted
to be pregnant
but hadn't wanted
to be fat.

So she'd taken slimming
pills. At the funeral everyone
said how well she looked.
Considering.

MASS HYSTERIA

With their fervent faith strengthened
By close calls to Kingdom come
The past behind them lengthened
Along a setting heatless sun.

Singing songs and saying prayers
For themselves and not each other
They were at early morning mass
To catch God's eye.

Side stepping neatly down the line
Of kneeling seekers after truth
The priest slipped the slivers slickly
Onto each protruding tongue.

The surrogate flesh devoured
Washed down the hopeful holy throats
With blood like medicine soured
By thoughts of an absent God.

Filled with conveyor belt comfort
This rheumy eyed cynical throng
So sure they can get into Heaven
On the back of a prayer and a song.

JUST NAMES ON A LIST

It was explained that
the financial results were disliked
in the City. So the company had to become
fitter. Healthier. More profitable.
People had to go.
It started with a demand
for thirty names. A 10% head-count
it was called. Not a hit list.
Just names of people who could be released.

The first few names were easy.
The dead beats and the no hopers.
That's ten already.
Then the genuinely surplus.
Up to fifteen now, halfway there.

What about the difficult buggers?
That woman in Accounts
and that limping sod in the post room.
Get them down! Settle some scores!

Include that snotty secretary
and the caretaker who
thinks he owns the Car Park.
At twenty five the names ran out:
that should be enough.

Thirty means thirty. The City expects you
to find some more. Another two,
that guy who has been ill,
he'll be grateful and that other one
who's good at his job but has the crying
fits. He'll be glad of the rest.

Then there's the tea lady
who's surely over sixty
and will be happier at home.
People can get their own tea.
Pity we can't touch the Chairman's
chauffeur or his gardener so we'd
better have the graduate from Marketing.

He's too bright and would have
left anyway. He just wanted to use us.
We'd better be fair, put his girl friend
down as well. That's it. Thirty names.
They may have been people once
but now they are just names on a list
and for the moment
the City is happy.

A SOLDIER'S DEATH

The talk was of drowning in mud.
Not a soldier's death.
I don't know about that I thought.
Dead is dead. Someone said,
The flower of English youth,
And sighed, and sighed. *Yes,*
Millions died. I sighed,
What is this to do with me?
I want to be concerned,
To taste salt tears,
But I don't really care
It was all so long ago.

Death is painless now.
A slow draining of the blood
And a drip, drip of subsidised
Life. Leaving ever bigger spaces
Between the drops until one lands
On an empty space and is returned
Not known at this address.

IT USED TO GO LIKE THAT

Back in 1966 when Bob Dylan
Gave up acoustic guitar
And formed an electric band
The move from folk music

To the rock and roll culture
Puzzled and angered many.
It pleased a few, a lot
Just didn't care.

He gave no word of explanation
But justified the radical change
By saying "It used to go like
That and now it goes like this."

In 1988 when I gave up work
After almost thirty years
To read for a degree. To find
Time to read. And write.

To lay in the sun. Talk to my wife.
I answer questions about my life
By saying "It used to go like
That and now it goes like this."

NOW YOU CAN DO ALL OF THOSE THINGS

The soulless eyes
Glanced up at the clock
As the mirthless mouth
Trotted out the line
For the tenth time that day,
"It's not you who is redundant.
It's the job."
The mouth half swallowed a yawn.

Seeing the sullen shock
On the face opposite
He pressed on
"This is an opportunity,
Not a disaster. Now you can do
All of those things.
Buy that business.
Sail round the world."
His small and standard joke
As fat hands smacked the desk
To be encouraging and dynamic.
"How old are you anyway?"

The chair scraped back
As the man stood up.
"I'm fifty five,"
He said, "Today."

IN MY RED POPPIED BLUE MAC

I always went alone to the parade.
Walking across Corporation Field in my
red poppied blue mac I felt important.
At eleven o'clock the guns would crack
the world into silence.
With just the flag rope slapping
its solitary sound.
Two minutes to remember.

I remember the Last Post crackling
from the roof of the Station Hotel.
Filling me with delicious sadness.
People shuffling, free from the silence
but caught within their own space inside
the crowd. Desolate and held by dead
and younger hands.

"Fallen comrades," choked the old man
in the beret. Standing stiffly to
attention in the bright and sunlit square.
But seeing only mud to drown in
through his far and distant eyes.

After the parade had passed
old people went to the square
to lay their ghosts and memories.
A white cross and a poppy. Or a wreath.
Always a tear, sometimes a salute.

I always stayed to read the names and
to deepen my sadness. Then, turning up
the collar of my blue mac I walked home
the long way round.

THE CERTIFICATE

'This is to certify.' It's dated May 1965
He would have been 34 or 35 then.
I'm never sure whether he was older
by eleven years or ten.
The certificate meant a lot to him.
And his wife.

It's still in the tube it was posted in.
Why didn't he hang it on the wall?
It meant so much. Perhaps too much.
"That was an unlucky house." So our mother
said. So we buried him from our house.
Theirs anyway. I'd left.
Mind first. Then body.

His wife had died before. "Don't put her
name in the paper." So our mother said
as I wrote out the piece for the Daily Mail.
Telling the world of her spite.
Blaming the dead for the dead.
Denying him for one last time.

I've some of his books. Reference of course.
And his certificate.
Perhaps the books belonged to his wife.
The certificate is still in the tube.